The Wee Book of
GLASGOW TRAMS

T0204623

Tom Noble

Black & White Publishing

First published 2003
by Black & White Publishing Ltd
99 Giles Street, Edinburgh EH6 6BZ

ISBN 1 902927 96 6

Front cover – A pair of westbound Cunarder trams emerge into the sunshine
from the gloom of the railway bridge in Glasgow's Argyle Street, a city landmark known as
the Hielanman's Umbrella.

Back cover – Portrait of a tram driver, or motorman, on the platform of a
Standard tram. He is demonstrating a draught-excluding screen which has been fitted to the
car in a bid to improve crew comfort.

A CIP catalogue record for this book is available from The British Library.

Printed and bound in Spain by Bookprint, S.L., Barcelona

TOM NOBLE is a Glasgow journalist who confesses to being an enthusiast for railways. This
is coupled with an interest in most forms of transport – except, perhaps, aircraft and camels,
both of which, he claims, come into the category of 'they all look the same from a distance'.
Trams and nostalgia fit neatly with a further inevitable spin-off from studying railways . . .
a fascination with the industrial archaeology and social history of Glasgow.

INTRODUCTION

The tramcar served Glasgow faithfully for ninety years, from 1872 onwards. Ever since the first horse-drawn tram set out from St George's Cross to Eglinton Toll, Glaswegians have had an unashamed affection for them which reached a peak at the farewell procession of 1962 when 250,000 endured torrential rain to say their goodbyes. At its peak, the city's tramway system was a huge undertaking. By 1923 it employed more than 10,000 people, owned more than 1,000 trams and operated on over 200 miles of track. It even generated its own electricity at Pinkston Power Station in Port Dundas.

The demise of the trams was one of the early milestones in Glasgow's decade of upheaval. It was the 1960s that saw the start of the widespread elimination of the tenements, the obsession with multistorey living and the creation of the motorway network.

This book makes no attempt to be a history of the Glasgow tramcar. Instead, it is a reflection on how the tramcar has become a vehicle for nostalgia – an image associated with an era that has gone, a lifestyle that is but a memory and a cityscape that has vanished under concrete and tarmac. The pictures come from the extensive photographic archives of *The Herald*, *Sunday Herald* and *Evening Times*, held at their Glasgow offices. They have been selected to capture not only the chronology of the Glasgow trams but also the life and times of the people who worked on the cars and used them on a daily basis.

Tom Noble

This is Jamaica Bridge – otherwise known as Glasgow Bridge – in 1893, with two of the Glasgow Tramway and Omnibus Company's horse-drawn trams jostling for space with other slow-moving traffic. The St Enoch Station Hotel, which opened in 1879, is prominent in the background to the right. The large poster for the Gaiety Theatre, in front of which is a boy in bare feet, announces the appearance of Fannie Leslie, celebrated burlesque artiste and vocalist who was apparently engaged at a very high fee. Marie Lloyd, another big star of the times, is not bottom of the bill, as it may appear, but the main attraction for the following week. At the top of the advertising hoardings is a sign with the immortal words:

They come as a boon and a blessing to men
The Pickwick, the Owl, and the Waverley Pen.

This was an advertisement for pen nibs and another, situated at the bottom of the approach road to St Enoch Station, survived into the 1960s.

4

This is thought to be the only photograph in existence of this particular type of horse-drawn tram. It is unique in that it has been fitted with leaf-type springs instead of the more usual coil springs – and linked Central Station and the Glasgow International Exhibition of 1888, which was held in Kelvingrove Park. For this official photograph, which was probably taken at Bluevale Depot, the car has been deliberately derailed to provide a side-on view.

The 1888 exhibition was opened by the Prince and Princess of Wales on 8 May and Queen Victoria paid two visits before it closed on 12 November, the event having attracted 5.7 million visitors. The Moorish-style buildings designed by architect James Sellars – who sadly died aged forty-four during the exhibition's run – were all demolished, but the Doulton Fountain was presented to the city and moved to Glasgow Green, where it has had a chequered existence.

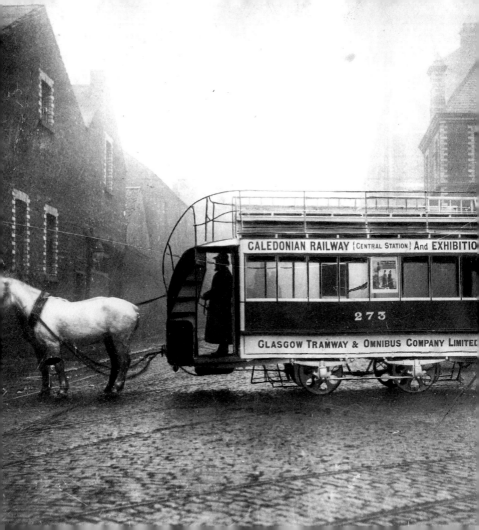

A westbound tram heads along Sauchiehall Street in the 1930s, past the legendary Empire Theatre. Dating from 1897, the Empire was a music hall-type venue whose weekend audiences gained a fearsome reputation, especially among English comedians. Des O'Connor has told how he appeared there early in his career and pretended to faint in order to get off the stage. Mike and Bernie Winters did no better, and even Morecambe and Wise walked off to the sound of their own footsteps. International stars such as Frank Sinatra, Danny Kaye and Judy Garland, however, did win over the notoriously difficult audiences and, in 1959, Cliff Richard had problems of a different kind when police had to control his screaming fans.

The Empire, situated between West Nile Street and Renfield Street, closed in 1963 (no doubt to the relief of the theatrical profession) and was replaced by a shop and office development called Empire House.

The horse-drawn trams dating from 1872 terminated just past this junction between Great Western Road and Kirklee Road and, on electrification, the tracks were extended westward through Anniesland and Knightswood in stages, although it was not until 1949 that Blairdardie was reached.

Here Standard tram No. 651 swings across into Kirklee Road on a wet day in the 1950s. According to contemporary newspaper reports, this was one of the city's most dangerous junctions at that time, with twenty-four accidents in a six-month period. It is not known how many were attributed to right-turning tramcars, though.

Despite how it looks, the cyclist in the photo is not really on a collision course with the tram, as they are well separated. Of course, he could fall victim to what in those days was every cyclist's nightmare – getting your wheels stuck in the tramlines.

This is Glasgow Cross, with the readily identifiable Tolbooth Steeple about the only part of the scene still in place. Work has begun on the Glasgow Central Railway, much of which was in tunnels, but the street-level building of Glasgow Cross Station which was eventually situated next to where the horse-drawn trams are positioned has not been started. This dates the picture to the early 1890s. Constructing a railway under busy city streets with the minimum of disruption was no easy task. The Glasgow Central Railway took 6 years, 25,000 tons of steel, 70 million bricks and a huge amount of cash. The statue of King William on a horse was moved further up the Trongate and then, in the 1930s, relocated to Castle Street.

A wet day in the Trongate in 1962 sees Coronation tram No. 1260 heading for Dalmuir West, with a uniformed policeman standing on the rear platform. Immediately behind the train, carrying an advertising sign for Red Hackle whisky, is Glasgow Cross Station, a simpler 1920s replacement for the original octagonal structure designed by architect John Burnet. The station closed in 1964 but the building was not demolished until 1977 and a raised flat area in the middle of Trongate marks the spot. Beyond that is the imposing 1920s Mercat Building, which has been suggested as a possible site for a railway station on the High Street–Shields line which runs behind it – if and when this reopens to passengers as part of a wider Glasgow Crossrail scheme. Trongate itself has suffered a decline in fortunes and is ripe for regeneration; better transport links should be an integral part of this.

The huge arched roof of Queen Street Station dominates this 1950s view of George Square, photographed from the south side as trams ferry their passengers along remarkably clear streets. The Glasgow firm of P. & W. MacLellan was responsible for the glazed structure, which dates from about 1880 and was part of the rebuild of the original 1842 terminus. The property immediately in front of the train shed has been replaced by a modern structure that extends across the station entrance and features that hallmark of 1970s railway architecture – white tiles more suited to a public toilet.

The hotel building to the right was on George Square before the railway was built and is still in business. Now known as the Millennium Hotel, it has also been called the Copthorne, the North British and the Queen's. The Merchants' House building on the corner looks much the same today and a galleon and globe still crown its dome.

In 2000 the George Square area was controversially resurfaced in a red material, resulting in the nickname 'Red Square'. Note the city skyline – no multistorey blocks to be seen.

By the mid-1930s Glasgow was in desperate need of modern tramcars that could run to the desired schedules. Authority was given to construct two experimental prototypes and the first of these, No. 1141, was unveiled at the beginning of January 1937. It was unlike anything that had gone before in terms of exterior styling and interior fittings.

This was the first tramcar to have forced ventilation and the grilles can be seen above the windscreen in this launch photograph. They were quickly hooded over when it was found they also admitted rainwater. The second prototype, No. 1142, was even more striking as it was painted in a special livery of silver, red and blue to mark the forthcoming coronation of King George VI. It was dubbed the 'Coronation' tram and the name stuck for the 100 production examples that were built by the Coplawhill Works. They featured prominently in publicity material for the Empire Exhibition held in Bellahouston Park from May to October 1938, but obviously did not carry as many visitors as was hoped. The exhibition organisers had predicted an attendance total of 20 million; the actual figure during a cold and wet summer was 12.5 million.

This is an obviously posed publicity photograph of the interior of the top deck of No. 1141, in which efforts have been made to portray a cross-section of the travelling public, albeit all male. Perhaps women did not frequent the top deck. A bowler hat, as worn by the man on the right, was not only the prerogative of the chief clerk or city gent, it was also a badge of office of senior management in shipyards, who probably did not use public transport. The seat backs are, of course, hinged in order that they can be reversed at the end of a journey. Many a small boy took great delight in running along the top deck on arrival at a terminus, pushing over the seat backs with a succession of satisfying clanks.

The coronation of King George VI in 1937 provided an excuse for the tramways department to produce this float representing the liner Queen Mary. *It was based on a works car, as were almost all of the mock-ups and specially decorated trams. In 1937 there was also a float portraying Henry Bell's* Comet, *a tram advertising the coronation carnival at Hampden Park and two which had been turned into a thatched cottage and a modern villa. Illuminated trams were popular right up until 1959, when one was used to promote the Scottish Industries Exhibition at the Kelvin Hall.*

Despite displaying route No. 26 – which ran from Dalmarnock to Scotstoun/Clydebank/Dalmuir West – Coronation tram 1274 is about to cross the Atlantic Ocean. Glasgow Corporation Transport donated this 1940-built tram to the Seashore Trolley Museum in Maine, USA, and it left Scotland aboard the US freighter, American Scientist, *bound for Boston.*

The loading operation at Glasgow's Meadowside Quay appears to have attracted a large audience of ships' crew and dockers – and not one hard hat among them. Standard tram No. 488 is also preserved outside the UK – as a static exhibit in the Paris Transport Museum.

In 1953–4 Glasgow Corporation bought forty-six trams from Liverpool to replace some of its ageing Standard trams. Costing £500 each, they were delivered by road, and here we see the first of them arriving at the Coplawhill Works in September 1953 on a Pickfords trailer. The incomers were known in Glasgow as Green Goddesses and were two feet longer than the home-grown equivalents, causing clearance problems which restricted them to two routes: the No. 29, Broomhouse–Milngavie (later Maryhill), service and the No. 15, Baillieston–Anderston Cross, service.

Experience demonstrated that, although longer in length, they were short on reliability and were plagued by electrical and bodywork problems. Crews also disliked them as they seated seventy-eight passengers – fourteen more than a conductor was accustomed to. Consequently, the Goddesses became unloved, unkempt and unwanted and were all withdrawn by 1960 – presumably becoming unmissed as well.

In September 1939 a reader of the now-defunct Glasgow newspaper The Bulletin *was experimenting with a newly purchased camera. He took this atmospheric and evocative picture on the top deck of a tram using only the available light and has captured a cross-section of the travelling public.*

One can only speculate as to the nature of the conversation the conductor is having with the well-dressed couple. His expression is somewhat stern – surely they are not trying to skip their fares? He could, of course, have been discussing the impending prospect of war because, within days, Neville Chamberlain was to make his now-famous radio broadcast and hostilities began. A blackout was imposed which would have meant there would have been no available light for The Bulletin *reader's picture, so it is fortunate that he took it when he did. He is unlikely to have made much use of his camera in the ensuing six years as film and opportunity were not easy to obtain during wartime.*

Wartime censorship has meant that details surrounding this picture of a bombed tramcar are sparse. It is car No. 6, which is listed as being scrapped in May 1941.

The location is thought to be Nelson Street in the Gorbals. There is certainly a recorded case of a group of cub scouts from a troop in the Gorbals being killed when the tramcar in which they were travelling was hit by a bomb in the early years of the Second World War.

This may or may not be the same tragic incident. And it is not an isolated example of the damage inflicted by enemy aircraft: photographs taken after the Clydebank blitz of March 1941 show trams at the Dalmuir Terminus reduced to mere shells. Bombing raids demonstrated the superiority of buses in getting people moving again quickly, as trams could not be utilised until damaged tracks were restored. Although Clydebank has become enshrined in history, areas such as Partick, Hyndland and Greenock were also victims of German bombers. After May 1941, Hitler turned his attention to Russia, and Scotland reaped the benefit.

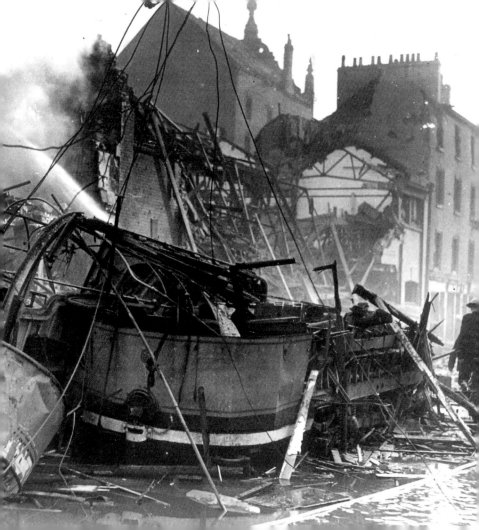

Fifty people were injured, two of them seriously, in this 1947 accident which was apparently caused by the brakes on Standard tram No. 643 failing as it was heading down Bilsland Drive towards Maryhill Road. It was unable to negotiate the tight right-hand turn at the aqueduct which carries the Glasgow branch of the Forth and Clyde canal and came off the rails, smashing into a wall.

The photograph was taken from the canal bank and, decades later, the road layout is unchanged. The tram, operating circular service No. 33, would have started its journey from the Hawthorn Street Terminus in Springburn, having sat between duties outside the 'new' Boundary Bar. This 1939-built hostelry, on the corner of Hawthorn Street and Springburn Road, was an exercise in chrome and walnut and featured opaque glass windows etched with bus and tramcar images.

The question which immediately springs to mind on seeing this photograph is: do all of these people have nothing better to do? Depending on the time of day, the streets could simply have been busy, or some of the onlookers could have been passengers on the trams involved in this incident at the corner of Hope Street and Argyle Street outside Central Station in October 1951. The tram carrying the advertisement for Vernons Pools is certainly off the rails and it would appear that the overhead wires have been damaged as two tower wagons are already in attendance. Beside the rear of the ambulance, a disconsolate tram driver appears to be discussing events with a couple of inspectors.

The ambulance itself is a real period piece – a Humber in two-tone brown livery. Ambulances in Scotland were later painted blue until the transition to white in the late 1960s.

*There were not many single-track sections in Glasgow
but the one which ran along Pleasance Street provided a
short-cut between the Newlands Tram Depot and
Pollokshaws. On a May evening in 1952 the inevitable
happened – two trams met in a head-on collision.
It is to be hoped that the drivers had time to jump
out before the impact.*

*Glasgow trams were designed to retain maximum
strength in the main passenger areas and the relatively
undamaged saloons of these two are a tribute to that.
The advertisement on the right-hand tram, headed
'Royal Salute', is not for a brand of whisky but for a
Boys' Brigade event at Ibrox Stadium at which the
guest of honour, according to the poster, was to be the
Prince of the Netherlands.*

A drawback that trams shared with trains was that one stoppage could have an unfortunate domino effect. The leading car in this rather long line in Sauchiehall Street in 1957 has had its front end remodelled, which suggests a collision. There appears to be remarkably little traffic coming up on the inside – unless, of course, there is something parked next to the pavement farther back up the street. The block on the left between Hope Street and Wellington Street is largely unchanged apart from the shops but, while the street at this point can still be teeming with pedestrians, there is no traffic.

In February 1954 a Standard tram on route No. 26 waits to proceed on its journey into the unknown, as least as far as Burnside. Smog was an early twentieth-century word describing what was chiefly a nineteenth-century creation. In certain weather conditions smoke from countless industrial and domestic chimneys combined with fog to produce a soot-laden, almost impenetrable blanket. The Great London Smog of 1952 lasted for five days and was responsible for 4,000 deaths. It resulted in the 1956 Clean Air Act, which created smokeless zones in which only smokeless fuel could be burnt.

Fog could be lethal in other ways too. In January 1959 two passengers and the driver died when an electrical fire swept through a tramcar in Old Shettleston Road, Glasgow, following a collision in fog with a lorry. The city's fire-master described the tragedy as a 'freak accident'.

Tram drivers could drop sand on to the rails ahead of the wheels to improve the adhesion in damp or frosty weather, although it is doubtful if sand would have had much effect in white-out conditions such as these. The lorry-like works car in this February 1947 scene was one of two specially built for transporting sand from the drier in Admiral Street to the various tram depots.

The Standard trams, with their open platforms, afforded less protection from the elements than their streamlined cousins but at least their top decks were eventually enclosed.

The procession of trams in both this photograph and the next makes it easy to understand why there was a groundswell of criticism about their inflexibility and contribution to the slow progress of city-centre traffic. This is the junction of Argyle Street and Jamaica Street, once known as Simpson's Corner after the drapery business of Robert Simpson and Sons that amalgamated with Arnott's in 1936 to form Arnott-Simpson. The shop shown here was destroyed by fire in 1951. A new Arnott-Simpson store was built on the original block in the 1960s (although it did not include the Jamaica Street corner site) and this served Glasgow shoppers until 1994, when the House of Fraser group sold it to a property company, which split it into separate retail units. At about the same time, Glasgow also lost other retail giants such as Lewis's, Goldberg's and Bremner's.

For several years in the 1950s one of Glasgow's main shopping areas was marred by this eyesore, which can only be described as a hole in the ground. This is Simpson's Corner again, now derelict as a result of the 1951 fire that destroyed half of the Arnott-Simpson store complex. Glasgow Corporation, which owned the land, finally agreed a lease deal with a developer but, by July 1957, the city fathers were getting fed up with the lack of progress – the reason this photograph was taken. Eventually Beaverbrooks, the jeweller, occupied the corner site until it gave way to a fast-food outlet. Examination of the shops over the road reveals a who's who of 1950s and '60s high-street names – like Timpson Shoes, Burton the Tailors, John Collier ('the window to watch', according to the TV advertising jingle), Treron and H. Samuel.

A cynic might observe that, in twenty-first-century Union Street, a similar scene to this could be recreated with buses any day of the week. It is June 1955 and trams are at a standstill due to an electricity supply problem. However, the enforced wait does give the crews the opportunity for a chat in the sunshine.

The properties housing Boots the Chemist, which proclaims itself open day and night, were replaced in the 1970s by a purpose-built store at the corner of Union Street and Argyle Street, a striking building which rapidly became dated and lasted only about twenty years. It was a favourite place for couples to meet for a night out – or to be stood up, as the case may be. This was known as 'getting a dissy'. About halfway along the line of trams, the nineteenth-century warehouses include the A-listed Egyptian Halls by the celebrated Glasgow architect Alexander 'Greek' Thomson.

Several routes funnelled through Bridgeton Cross so it would not take long for tramcars to stack up in the event of a power supply failure – which is what has happened again in this scene from December 1959. To the right of the leading vehicle, where the kilted gentleman with the briefcase is standing, is Bridgeton Central Railway Station, a busy terminus for trains from Helensburgh and Balloch. It was also part of the network of unadvertised rail services that transported hundreds of Clydeside workers. It became part of the electrified Blue Train network in 1960 and ceased to be a passenger station in 1979 when the Glasgow Central low-level line reopened with a station near Bridgeton Cross. Ironically, the tunnel for this line follows London Road and is therefore immediately underneath these trams. Bridgeton Central was a cleaning depot for electric trains until replaced by a new facility at Yoker in 1987, but the on-street building still exists as a betting shop.

Eglinton Street was a major south-side bottleneck,
especially in the morning as traffic headed for the city.
It could therefore be some time before Standard tram
No. 713 reaches the comparative serenity of the
Bishopbriggs terminus in Kenmure Avenue. This
photograph must have been taken in the late 1950s as
tram service No. 25 ended on 6 June 1959. The bus,
which looks relatively new, is a Daimler dating from 1955.
Just one question: how can this bus be going to Pollok
if it is heading north along Eglinton Street? The
places on its destination screens are in the opposite
direction. Perhaps it is empty, going from a garage to the
city-centre terminus in Midland Street and already
displaying its next destination.

The Fordson tipper lorry in the foreground is owned by
Alexandra Transport, a major haulage company in
Glasgow in the 1950s and 1960s, which was based in
Alexandra Parade, Dennistoun.

It has been claimed that the name Auchenshuggle was an invention of Glasgow Corporation Transport. Here, a Coronation tram heads for there having just emerged from the Hielanman's Umbrella – formed when Central Station was built over Argyle Street and artificially lit, even in daytime. This is a Glasgow institution and Highlanders exiled in the city traditionally gathered here of a Saturday evening, sheltering from the elements. Each island group would meet outside a particular shop, exchange gossip and presumably move on to somewhere more convivial.

To the left of tram No. 1372, on a lamp-post, is a blue British Railways sign pointing to 'River Steamers'. This refers to the Caledonian Steam Packet Company ships which left from Bridge Wharf on the south bank of the river at Clyde Place. A day sail to Tighnabruaich and back on the Queen Mary II *was a favourite excursion for Glaswegians in the 1950s and '60s. The steamer returned at about 8 p.m. and the fare was 10 shillings, the equivalent of 50p today. Today, Clyde steamers have no administrative links with the railways; city streets are not cobbled; and tobacco companies are not allowed to advertise in this manner.*

*Between 1948 and 1952 Glasgow Corporation Transport's
Coplawhill Works built 100 cars which were based on the
highly successful pre-war Coronation design but with
differences in their interior layout and bogie design. They
became known as 'Cunarders' and it is appropriate that
one was photographed in Clydebank, passing the office
block of John Brown's shipyard.*

*This was the birthplace of countless vessels – including
the four Cunard sister liners,* Saxonia, Ivernia, Corinthia
and Sylvania, *whose dome-topped funnels may have given
the tramcars their nickname – and the famous Cunarders,
the* Queen Mary, Queen Elizabeth *and* QE2. *The shipyard
was also responsible for creating the Clydebank
community and even its very name when, in the 1870s,
the Thomson brothers relocated their Clyde Bank shipyard
from Govan to a green-field site at the confluence of the
Cart and Clyde that allowed even the biggest ships to be
launched safely. In 1899 the yard was acquired by
Sheffield armour-plating maker John Brown & Co. Ltd.
The last reminders of the yard's history were auctioned off
in April 2002 and the 78-acre site cleared. A crane was
retained as a memorial to an illustrious past.*

The canal bridge at Blairdardie had proved an insurmountable obstacle to tramcar routes being extended any farther along Great Western Road, but no such difficulty appears to have been encountered at Clydebank where, for a quarter of a century, single-decker trams on the Kilbowie Road–Duntocher service crossed the Forth and Clyde canal. Known locally as the 'wee caurs', single-deckers were required because of two low railway bridges in Kilbowie Road and, when the service began in 1924, ex-Paisley District Tramways cars were used. The wee caurs survived until December 1949, when they were replaced by buses. Kilbowie Road still crosses the Forth and Clyde canal but there the resemblance ends; almost everything in this scene has gone. Modern planners made a better job of obliterating old Clydebank than the Luftwaffe did in 1941.

The two World Wars of the twentieth century saw women playing an ever-increasing role in industries such as shipbuilding, engineering and munitions, carrying out work which had hitherto been the exclusive preserve of men. They were not universally welcomed, terms like 'the dilution of labour' indicating how they were viewed by trade unions. Most women had to give up their jobs as soon as hostilities ended to make way for men returning from the armed forces.

Glasgow introduced women tram drivers during the First World War as a result of manpower shortages, but continued the practice during peacetime and until the end of trams in the city. This 1951 intake of recruits is being introduced to the basic principles of tramcar driving by Chief Instructor Harry Drewett. In the days before computerised simulators, sets of dummy controls and miniature traffic lights were as far as technology would stretch. It is not known if recordings of appropriate sounds were played at these classes.

After basic instruction, trainee tram drivers progressed to the next stage – actually driving a tram. The Motor School used single-decker No. 1017, which had originally been open-top double-decker No. 17 in the Paisley fleet, acquired by Glasgow when it took over the system in 1923. It was an everyday sight shuttling up and down a single track in Coplaw Street, which ran from Pollokshaws Road, across Victoria Road to Cathcart Road and was not used for public services. No. 1017 carried the legend 'School Car', but this did not refer to transporting children. The Motor School also had a static tram skeleton, with all the electrical components and wiring exposed to demonstrate how a tramcar works. The school closed in about 1960 and the body of No. 1017 spent some thirty years as a summerhouse in a garden before being moved to Summerlee Heritage Museum in Coatbridge, where it was painstakingly restored and given a replacement truck from Lisbon.

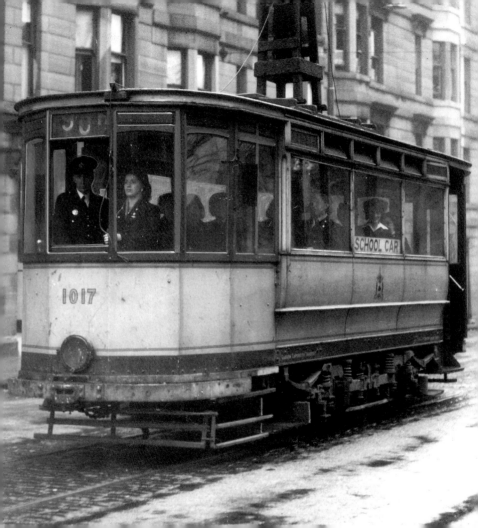

Would-be tram conductresses and conductors were given their training at the Corporation's transport department office in Govan, where they were introduced to the intricacies of the ticket machine. Of course, issuing tickets was only part of the job. Keeping the passengers in order was a major facet, although this is unlikely to have been a big feature of 1950s induction programmes. The widely held perception of the no-nonsense Glasgow tram conductress was recognised in 1991 by the National Museum of Science and Industry in London, no less. The museum had a drama programme in which it proclaimed: 'History comes to life with actors/interpreters inspiring children to learn about such colourful characters as Amy Johnson (Gypsy Moth); Thomas Crapper of flush loo fame; Bridie McPherson, the Glasgow tram conductress –' Bridie who? When quizzed, the museum admitted they had made up the Bridie character but that she was 'based on extensive research into the working lives of women on the trams'. Bridie's character was 'ebullient, outgoing, extrovert and strong' and her script included her having to cope with Glasgow drunks and recalcitrant urchins. Will the real Bridie McPherson please stand up?

'Look, there's a man taking our picture. Has he never seen anybody get off a tram before?' That may or may not have been what was going through the minds of this couple as they leave a No. 25 bound for Carnwadric from Bishopbriggs on the other side of the city. This photograph just speaks 1950s and not only because of the tram. The woman on the left carrying her purchases in a net bag is also holding a cardboard box, which may contain cakes from the City Bakeries, perhaps. A headscarf, such as that worn by the woman boarding the tram, is now a thing of the past. So, too, are slogans like the advertisement on the side of the tram – undoubtedly true in the 1950s when smoking was perceived as being sophisticated. Perhaps sophistication did not motivate the man in the bunnet. Maybe he just liked a fag.

After tram routes 1 and 30 were replaced by buses in 1960, Glasgow's Great Western Road had no further requirement for the tracks and they were ripped up, a process which made its own contribution to traffic disruption. Redundant tramlines were not always removed; sometimes they were simply tarred over.

This photograph was taken near that notorious junction of Great Western Road and Kirklee Road, this time looking towards Anniesland. To the right of the traffic lights once stood a West End institution: a post office in a wooden shed that defied the march of progress until 2001, when it was replaced by a modern unit. The bus in the distance is a Glasgow Corporation AEC Regent working the No. 19 service from Clydebank to George Square.

Auchenshuggle terminus was in London Road near Carmyle, and this view shows a Coronation and a Cunarder about to begin the journey to Dalmuir. The last scheduled tram to run in Glasgow was a No. 9 from Dalmuir West to Auchenshuggle on 2 September 1962. Thereafter, a special service operated from Anderston Cross to Auchenshuggle at a flat fare of sixpence for any distance, which included a souvenir pink ticket. Just before 6 p.m. on 4 September 1962 Coronation tram No. 1174, which had operated the last of these special trips, arrived at Dalmarnock depot and an era ended.

Dalmuir West Terminus, the other end of the No. 9 route from Auchenshuggle, was in Dumbarton Road, Dalmuir, at the junction with Mountblow Road. These two trams, a Coronation nearer the camera and a Cunarder behind, were almost at the end of their working lives when photographed here on a dismal day in August 1962. The large brick building in the background has gone, having been replaced by a church. However, the location's transport history lives on in the name of a local shop – The Terminus Store.

The transport elements of this view of Dumbarton Road effectively date the photograph. The double-arrow logo on the railway bridge was part of the corporate rebranding that accompanied Glasgow's suburban electrification. This was inaugurated in November 1960 and introduced the famous Blue Trains. The last tram on this route ran in September 1962, so the photograph was taken between these dates. It is difficult to work out why it was taken at all, unless to illustrate the impending demise of the trams. The Ford Anglia approaching the camera is straddling the tramlines leading into Hayburn Street, where the Partick Tram Depot was located. The railway station, originally known as Partick, was renamed Partick Hill in the 1950s when the buildings were replaced by brick and concrete structures. These survived as railway offices after a new station and interchange with the Underground was opened nearby in 1979, reviving the name of Partick.

Even by Townhead's standards, this is a traffic jam to reckon with. This stretch of Castle Street, going south from Parliamentary Road past the junctions with Alexandra Parade and Stirling Road and continuing to High Street and Glasgow Cross, was a notorious bottleneck by the early 1960s and progress was invariably slow in what is laughingly termed the rush hour. The city planners' solution was to demolish everything in this scene and replace it with motorway flyovers and junctions. Today's motorist, stuck in a snarl-up outside the Royal Infirmary, could be forgiven for thinking that some things never change.

Travellers on this diverse selection of public transport vehicles will have had plenty of time to read that the Casino's main feature was Loser Takes All, *starring Glynis Johns and Rossano Brazzo. Immediately opposite was another picture house, the Carlton, which had a memorial to three Covenanter martyrs built into one wall. Rivals for decades, the two cinemas closed within a year of each other in 1965-6, the Casino having a short career as a bingo hall before joining the Carlton as a victim of the rampaging bulldozer.*

St Vincent Street in March 1960 and a Standard tram
en route to Anniesland turns right for the climb up
Renfield Street in service No. 30's last year. It has just
passed Daniel Brown's, a renowned eatery in its day and
now, like so many of its contemporaries, a piece of
history. The same could be said of the car passing it, an
almost-new French Renault Dauphine. Foreign cars were
not that common in Glasgow in those days but one of
the first Renault dealers was Wylie and Lochhead, in
Berkeley Street near Charing Cross. Their premises were
demolished in the mid-1990s. The Dauphine was
introduced into Britain to the accompaniment of
advertising which extolled its road-holding virtues. Alas,
heavy in the rear and light in the front, it gained a
reputation for being anything but stable. As one critic
put it, 'A Dauphine could change lanes in a crosswind
all on its own.'

The early hours of 22 March 1961 was a busy time for fire-fighters in the east end of Glasgow. A blaze which broke out in the roof of Dalmarnock Tramcar Depot in Ruby Street quickly spread to the rest of the building – which contained a high proportion of timber and paint – and staff were hurriedly evacuated. Flames leaped a hundred feet into the air as fire crews fought to contain the blaze and prevent it from spreading to nearby tenements, where families were warned to leave their homes. As the battle went on, flames were seen about half a mile away. A sawmill in London Road was also ablaze and it too was threatening nearby houses. The tram depot fire was finally brought under control by about 2 a.m. and daylight revealed the full extent of the damage and the fact that fifty tramcars had been destroyed. Ironically, they included No. 108, seen here as a twisted shell, which had been earmarked for preservation. The roofless building continued in use until the end of the trams a year later.

A driver's-eye view of the stretch of Argyle Street west of Hope Street as two trams are about to pass. As the woman and two children to the left of the Ford Anglia have not started to move into the centre of the road, they must be waiting for a bus service that shares the stop with the trams.

Some of the properties in this 1962 view have survived but, by 2003, the block on the immediate left had been demolished and replaced by flats. The Central Station bridge ahead, carrying the Schweppes advertisement, is still with us. It is easy to forget how extensive cobbled city streets were in those days, and the tramways department was responsible for maintaining the granite setts between the rails and for eighteen inches on each side. Much of the maintenance of the system was carried out at night using specialist works tramcars which rarely saw the light of day. The permanent way yard was at Barrland Street, behind Pollokshaws Road and opposite the Coplawhill Works.

When this photograph was taken in 1962, this was said to be the only tree in Argyle Street and moves were made to ensure its survival. The location is 1223 Argyle Street at the junction with Gray Street, and the leafy landmark is being passed by an eastbound Coronation tram on service No. 9. More than forty years later the tree is still there. However, it can no longer claim to be the only one in Argyle Street as pedestrianisation of the city centre has resulted in decorative trees – none of which are the size of this one.

Anderston Cross was once the centre of a bustling district, thronged with shoppers by day and alive with public house and chip shop clientele by night. Now, like so much of old Glasgow, it is under a motorway.

The Anderston Cross Railway Station site was reborn with the inauguration of the Argyle Line through Glasgow Central low level in 1979, but street access is now from an island in a sea of roads below the Kingston Bridge.

The original station, which closed to passengers in August 1959, included the curved two-storey street-level ticket office on the left of this picture. Outside it was the terminus of the No. 15 Anderston Cross–Baillieston tram service, which outlasted the trains by eighteen months before being replaced by the No. 62 bus.

With a working life of only weeks ahead of it, Coronation tram No. 1189 heads east through Anderston Cross and along Argyle Street on service No. 9 on a wet day in August 1962.

*The end of Glasgow's trams came on the evening of
4 September 1962, with an emotional parade through
the city witnessed by an estimated 250,000 people.*

*In the lead was the horse-drawn double-decker tram
No. 543, pulled by two white horses borrowed, with their
driver, from St Cuthbert's Co-operative Society in
Edinburgh. This dictated the speed of the procession, so
it was sedate. The route from Dalmarnock Tram Depot in
Ruby Street was by way of London Road, Trongate,
Argyle Street (where it is pictured passing Lewis's
department store), Hope Street, St Vincent Street,
Renfield Street, Union Street, Jamaica Street, Eglinton
Street and Albert Drive. Here the passengers
disembarked, before the cars went into the Coplawhill
Works, empty but with their lit interiors emitting that
familiar welcoming glow. Their lights were about to be
extinguished permanently.*

Many of the passengers on the last trams came away with souvenirs, some with the help of a screwdriver. But, for the watching crowd, the best memento was a penny pressed into shape under a tram's wheels. This man is doing just that but, as the cars we see heading along Trongate are going away from the camera, it will be the one on which the photographer is standing that will do the needful. As it happens, this was No. 779. Some enterprising onlookers have taken up position on the roof of the Glasgow Cross Railway Station building, which is the structure carrying the Irn-Bru advertisement.

The second tram in the farewell procession was No. 672, one of the 'room and kitchen' cars. These had two saloons – one of which was left unglazed for smokers and separated from the other by a central entrance – and took their nickname from the traditional tenement flat. They were used on the Mitchell Street–Springburn route which, in view of its hilly nature, was the first to be electrified. A plaque marking the centenary was unveiled in October 1998 outside a restaurant in Mitchell Street. On its historic last passenger-carrying journey, No. 672 was driven by the longest-serving driver and carried Glasgow's Lord Provost, Jean Roberts, on the driver's left, as well as the transport department's General Manager, Eric Fitzpayne. It had survived as a mains testing car and had been rebuilt to near original condition before this event, with a view to its going on show in the proposed Museum of Transport. The car is pictured in Union Street passing the Boots store where, as can be seen from the cobbles, it was now seriously raining.

In the late 1950s Glasgow Corporation's transport and museums departments discussed the possibilities of preserving something of the city's tramcar heritage. Horse-drawn tram No. 543, which had been set aside some years earlier, and the old 'room and kitchen' tram No. 672 were obvious choices.

As part of the project, Standard tram No. 779 was restored to a 1908 style of bodywork and it is pictured in August 1962, near the Coplawhill Works where the transformation was carried out and where the trams earmarked for the museums department were stored pending a permanent home. In the event, this turned out to be the former paint shop at the Coplawhill Works, which became the city's first Museum of Transport. It was opened by the Queen Mother on 14 April 1964, just eighteen months after the trams had taken part in the farewell procession. The old paint shop found a new role as the Tramway Theatre when the Museum of Transport was relocated to the Kelvin Hall, with the seven trams in the city collection forming part of the exhibits.

The Glasgow Garden Festival, held at Prince's Dock in Govan, was opened by the Prince and Princess of Wales on 28 April 1988. The royal couple travelled on Glasgow tram No. 22, which had been brought back to its native city from the National Tramway Museum at Crich in Derbyshire. Five trams were used, and this is ex-Glasgow Cunarder No. 1297 – also from Crich – passing the Crystal Pavilion, created from 495 panes of glass and housing displays on the science of crystals.

The festival made good use of the river and canting basin, a former turning area for vessels, and a tramway and narrow-gauge railway took people around the extensive site. The event attracted four million visitors and injected much-needed cash into the city's economy.

More importantly, it acted as a springboard for Glasgow's efforts at repositioning itself as a tourist and conference city, becoming European City of Culture in 1990 and City of Architecture and Design in 1999.

One would have thought the end of the Second World War would have given Glasgow councillors enough to think about – like creating homes and employmen[t] However, some had a bee in their collective bonnet about trams with a separate e[xit] and entrance, so one was duly constructed and unveiled in 1947. It operated circular routes but the travelling public, being used to boarding at the rear, did n[ot] take to the front entrance. The locations were swapped over but the car, No. 100[5] was still restricted in where it could be used and, in 1956, it was converted to normal operation. Apparently, the lesson was not learned. In the early 1970s bus[es] with separate entrances and exits appeared on the streets of Glasgow. Similar vehicles were being successfully utilised in many other cities, speeding up passen[ger] flow. Not surprisingly, they did not last long in Glasgow.